MEN-AT-ARMS SERIES

EDITOR: MARTIN WINDROW

British Infantry Equipments 1908-80

Text and colour plates by

MIKE CHAPPELL

OSPREY PUBLISHING LONDON

Published in 1980 by
Osprey Publishing Ltd
Member company of the George Philip Group
12–14 Long Acre, London WC2E 9LP
© Copyright 1980 Osprey Publishing Ltd

ISBN 0 85045 375 5

Filmset in Great Britain
Printed in Hong Kong

Author's acknowledgements
My thanks are due to my wife, Marilyn, for her
assistance in researching this book and for typing the
manuscript. Except where otherwise stated the
photographs in this book were taken by Simon
Chappell and are copyright to him.

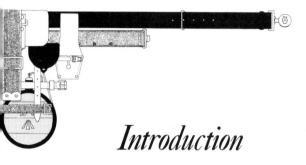

Introduction

One of the habits remaining after spending over 20 years in the British Army is that of determining an aim before setting out on even the most limited venture. Having settled on my aim in writing and illustrating this book, I feel I should declare it at the outset so that the reader may be in no doubt as to its scope.

This book deals with the personal equipment worn by the British infantryman since the early years of the 20th century. It has been written mainly to provide information for the military modeller, for the student of British military dress, and for the small but growing band of militaria collectors who acquire personal equipment. With this in mind I have concentrated on the equipment sets which saw service in combat with the infantry arm of the British Army. Experimental items have been excluded, but unofficial modifications by the soldier on service are shown where applicable.

I have striven to use the correct terminology wherever possible, and have only taken the liberty of reversing the Ordnance vocabulary's nomenclature in order to make a name more intelligible (e.g. combat pack and pistol case instead of 'Packs, field, combat' and 'Cases, pistol, W.E.'). Each of the seven sets covered has

been allocated a section, and each section begins with the historical background to the set before giving a thorough description of its construction. The 1937 pattern equipment warrants a longer section, as it had more variations and special items than any other set before or since. Concerning the equipment of the future, it must be remembered that the 1958 and 1944 pattern sets are still in service and that the equipment which may replace them is at the trials and development stage. In illustrating the final section I have therefore used a certain amount of licence based on available details of future developments.

The assembled '08 pattern Full Marching Order showing its 'one-piece' design.

An interesting photograph showing both '08 and '14 pattern being worn within the same unit. Here members of a Territorial battalion of the Devons use a German prisoner to help clear casualties and debris from a British trench. Note the 'shorts' worn by the figures in the foreground, forerunners of the Bombay bloomers of the next war; also the litter of '08 and '14 equipment items. (Imperial War Museum. All photographs not specifically credited to other sources are from the author's collection.)

A former commanding officer of mine, a soldier with a distinguished record in the Second World War, once said in a speech to recruits in 1952 that the job of the infantryman was to march, dig and shoot. An efficient infantryman, he declared, was one who could march, dig and shoot well. His summary of the rifleman's rôle those 27 years ago may seem almost totally redundant today, and especially so when set against the scenario of future wars; but I venture to suggest that there is still much to be said for this simple dictum. To be able to locate your enemy and shoot at him with effect is still the main task of the infantryman in battle, although the priority allocated to skill-at-arms training in peacetime sometimes makes one doubt it. Physical fitness or the ability to move on foot on the battlefield with a combat load is also a important today as it ever was; and I doubt if there will ever be a better defence against enemy fire than the pick and shovel! March, dig and shoot: and in order to do this, and to carry the load of ammunition, water and tools vital to the infantryman, mechanized or on foot, a well-designed set of personal equipment is as necessary today as it was in 1914. The weight of the combat load has certainly changed little in the intervening years.

When making a study of infantry equipment sets from the period of the Napoleonic wars to the present day one is bound to be struck by the way that good designs have been followed by bad ones, and by the way in which certain configurations repeat themselves after long absence. To give an example within the scope of this book one has only to note how some of the best design features of the 1908 pattern web equipment were apparently ignored when the replacement 1937 pattern was under development. The main charter of the team designing the 1937 pattern was to provide a method of carriage for the magazines of the Bren LMG. This could easily have been accomplished by modifying the 1908 pattern. Instead, an entirely new (and, in the case of the pack, ill-fitting) design was introduced, which saw service as the 1937 and 1944 patterns for over 20 years—until superseded by a superior design incorporating most of the best features of the 1908 pattern! Another example, if the reader studies the 1871 Valise Equipment featured in the companion volume *British Infantry Equipments 1808–1908*, is the strong similarity between the equipment sets of 1871 and 1958, both very good designs in their day. It is worth noting that both these sets were introduced after painstaking research and development. Nevertheless, no evidence exists that any serious attempt has ever been made to obtain the perfect solution from the 'customer', the infantryman. New designs have stemmed from committees as a result of the shortcomings of the current equipment sets, and have been presented to the soldier —like it or lump it. The quality of the design could then be gauged by the degree to which, given the opportunity, the soldier discarded or modified his equipment. In this one is reminded of the Union infantry of the American Civil War

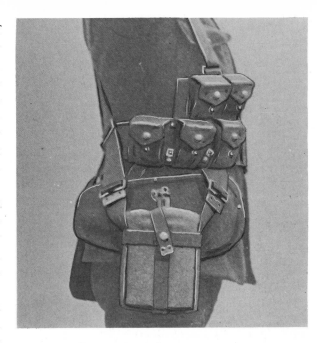

Right side of '08 pattern equipment, less pack.

Left side of '08 pattern equipment, less pack.

Front view of '08 pattern Marching Order worn unbuckled, to demonstrate the balance and comfort of the set while on the march.

Men of the 17th King's parade at Belton Park, Grantham, in June 1915. Typical of the 'Kitchener battalions' forming and training in the UK at this time, they are wearing the 'stopgap' 1914 leather equipment.

discarding their uncomfortable packs *en masse* in favour of the 'horseshoe roll' blanket as soon as the drill field receded and the battlefield loomed. Their Confederate counterparts rarely had packs to discard and were not noticeably less effective for that.

Yet another recurring theme is the contradiction between the loads carried in equipment sets at the design stage and when on actual service. Almost invariably the infantryman's maximum load was reckoned at the design stage as 40–45lb; and almost invariably the load on service has exceeded this, sometimes by as much as 50 per cent. This has been due in some instances to changing tactical dictates, as in the First World War, which saw the introduction of shrapnel helmets, respirators, grenades, etc.; but generally it can be ascribed to the practice of Regimental Standing Orders requiring items of clothing, cleaning equipment, etc., which are not vital to the fighting performance of the infantryman, to be carried into battle. Even today Combat Equipment, Fighting Order may require the infantryman to carry boot-brushes and polish, toilet articles, sewing kit, spare socks, pullover, poncho, cap comforter, mess-tins, knife, fork and spoon, weapon cleaning kit and sometimes a blanket. All this, in addition to ammunition and

weapon, respirator and NBC equipment, helmet, water, pick or shovel, and 24 hours' food! The tradition of the British soldier who shaves and shines in the face of the enemy dies hard, and it is, quite literally, a burdensome tradition. Even though most equipment sets were designed so that the wearer could remove and dump his small pack or its equivalent before battle, thus being left with the essentials of ammunition, water and tools, the opportunity to do so without the loss of the pack rarely occurs. Consequently the infantryman fights carrying the full list of razors, dubbin and so forth considered vital to his well-being by the promulgator of Standing Orders. In this respect little has changed since the days of Rifleman Harris, who, on disembarkation at Mondego Bay in 1808, 'marched under a weight sufficient to impede a donkey', and who, at the first opportunity, took the liberty of flinging part of his burden 'to the Devil'!

No record of infantry equipment in the 20th century would be complete without some reference to the Mills Equipment Company, who were responsible for the introduction of woven cotton webbing equipment into the armies of Great Britain and the United States. That webbing equipment is almost universal today is due, in the main, to this company, their US counterparts and their successors. Legend has it that the Mills Equipment Company owed its existence to an officer in the US Army in the days of the Indian Wars of the late 19th century. Captain Anson Mills, noting how the leather loops of the improvised cartridge belts in service at the time caused cartridges to corrode and stick, designed a belt using canvas loops which kept the ammunition serviceable and free. Determined to promote his ideas for webbing equipment, he went into partnership with a weaver and set up a factory to produce woven cotton webbing cartridge belts to a variety of designs. These belts were accepted by the US Army, and saw service in the campaigns of continental expansion and the Spanish-American Wars. Mills enlarged his operation and, in the first decade of the 20th century, the US Army took into service a set of equipment made entirely from cotton webbing.

The British Army had used Mills webbing bandoliers in the Boer War, but, because ammu-

Assembled '14 pattern Full Marching Order. Note the method of attachment of the pouches to the belt.

nition had been lost from them on the march, a low opinion of webbing was held in British military circles. Against this resistance it says much for the quality of design of the Mills 1908 pattern webbing equipment that it was accepted as a replacement for the leather infantry equipment then in service. The Mills Equipment Company in Great Britain never looked back from this moment, and went on to manufacture and supply webbing equipment to the British, British Empire and Commonwealth armed forces.

To conclude my introduction I feel that a few personal details may help to establish my credentials as a commentator on the subject, and may lend substance to various criticisms which will be found in my text. I served for 22 years in the British infantry, spending 19 of those years with the Gloucestershire Regiment. In that time I held every rank from Private to Warrant Officer Class One, and most appointments including RSM. Having left the service in 1974 I can claim personal experience of at least three of the equip-

Front view of the '14 equipment showing the 50-round cotton bandolier removed from the left pouch.

Rear view of the '14 pattern Full Marching Order.

ment sets covered in this book, in climates and countries ranging from the Far East through Africa and the Middle East to the usual garrisons in Germany and the UK. Whilst making no claim that my experience is unique, I do feel that it enables me to approach the subject with authority, and with a certain sympathy for the users of equipments outside my personal experience. In this latter category I have been able to draw on the experience and recollection of my father, grandfather, uncles and their comrades. They muster a catalogue of service dating from 1911 through both World Wars and most of the minor wars fought in the periods of 'world peace'. To them, and to all members of the British Army, past and present, I respectfully dedicate this book.

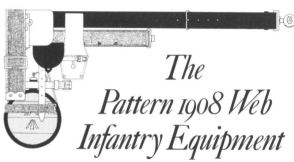

The Pattern 1908 Web Infantry Equipment

Historical

The conflict in South Africa from 1899 to 1902 gave the British military establishment reason to effect swift reforms in the period which followed the end of hostilities. The humiliating defeats suffered at the hands of a comparatively small number of Boer citizen-soldiers in the opening months of the war showed up deficiencies in leadership, training and equipment. Following a familiar pattern, and like a tough but inept boxer, the British took their bloody nose and eventually won on points in a long contest characterized by plenty of hard pounding but little skill. Victory brought opportunity to learn from mistakes, and infantry personal equipment was one of the items which came under scrutiny.

Experience showed the current Slade-Wallace equipment to be unsuitable for an infantry arm equipped with a charger-fed magazine rifle. Pro-

ision for the carriage of ammunition in chargers
(clips) was poor. The equipment was made from
material—buffalo hide—which might have
laddened the heart of a parade-ground enthu-
iast when pipeclayed, but which was unsuited
or the battlefield of the early 20th century. Most
elling of all, the design of the Slade-Wallace
quipment was bad. The valise, when worn,
ragged the belt upwards, and the greatcoat—
vorn rolled at the back of the belt—put undue
train on the hips. In South Africa the valise was
enerally discarded, and infantry fought and
narched without its badly-balanced weight. In
he reports of the 1903 Royal Commission on the
Var in South Africa we see the Slade-Wallace
quipment described as 'an absurdity', and, by
n infantry officer, as 'cumbersome, heavy and
adly balanced'.

**The 13th Durham LI waiting to put in an attack at the battle
of Menin Road Ridge, 20 September 1917. The four men
nearest the camera are wearing '08 pattern equipment; the
fifth and sixth men up the communication trench are wearing 1914 pattern leather. Evident in this photograph is the
battle load of the First World War infantryman in the attack:
note the digging tools, Lewis gun magazine panniers, extra
ammo in bandoliers and the items of personal kit tied to
packs. Most men turn from the intruding camera: much
can be read in the expression of the man who scowls at the
photographer. (Imperial War Museum)**

In providing an immediate replacement for
the equipment which had served our infantry so
badly the example of the recent enemy—the Boer
—was followed, and a leather bandolier equipment was taken into service. It is sufficient to say
of the 1903 Bandolier Equipment that it was
realized soon after its introduction that a better
designed equipment would be needed for the
infantryman.

9

In the years 1906–08 a committee to examine the diet, training and clothing of the soldier was set up under the chairmanship of the Surgeon-General. A design of infantry equipment produced by Major Burrowes of the Royal Irish Fusiliers, in collaboration with the Mills Web Equipment Company, was presented to the Equipment sub-committee for examination in 1906. The equipment found favour with the sub-committee and troop trials followed in Great Britain, the Middle East and India. As a result of these trials the Mills-Burrowes equipment was accepted by the Army Council in December 1907. Work was now put in hand to re-equip the infantry arm of the British Army with the equipment which would serve them through the Great War and the 20 years that followed. The official title given to the equipment was the pattern 1908 Web Infantry Equipment.

Description

The main feature of the Burrowes design was a diagonal strap passing from the rear of the ammunition pouches at the front of the wearer's body and downwards to the rear, where it attached to straps which passed around the valise or pack. This arrangement ensured that most of the weight in the pack bore down through the pouches and the braces supporting them, which were in turn connected to the upper edge of the pack. Thus the weight of the pack was distributed evenly, even when the ammunition pouches were empty.

1908 pattern valise or pack, showing attachment points to braces and pouches; and (right) detail of pouch showing three chargers in place, totalling 15 rounds.

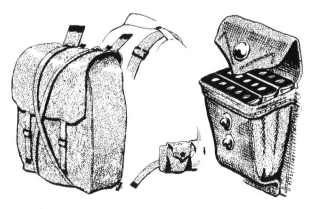

The assembled equipment was in one piece and could be put on and taken off like a coat, and—when properly adjusted to suit the wearer—the belt-buckles could be unfastened on the march for greater comfort and cooling.

For the first time there were no constricting straps across the chest, as the water-bottle and haversack were attached to the extremities of the braces. (It must be borne in mind that the water bottle and haversack had always been added as supplementary items to previous equipments sets. The 1908 pattern web equipment incorporated these items in the whole set.)

The woven cotton webbing from which the equipment was made represented an advance on the materials used before—tan leather or whitened buffalo hide. When wet, cotton webbing would still do the job it was designed for without serious discomfort or deterioration, whereas the properties of wet leather are well known. However, it was realized soon after the introduction of the 1908 pattern equipment that some form of renovator was needed to keep up the colouring of the webbing and—as always in the case of the British Army of the day—to preserve a smart appearance. A preparation in powder form was eventually approved which, when mixed with water, formed a paste which evenly coated the webbing with the colour desired. There were several shades of khaki green, blue and grey. The cleaner was unique in that, when dry, it gave the webbing a waterproof quality. Desirable though this was, it could lead to problems when the next coating of renovator came to be applied. Trying to dampen waterproofed webbing could be frustrating!

The buckles, studs and tags of the 1908 pattern equipment were all made of brass. All the buckles were of the 'D' design with a portion of the buckle frame cut out to permit quick release of the strap-end.

The 1908 pattern web equipment set consisted of:

One waistbelt (three inches wide).
Two braces (two inches wide).
Two cartridge carriers or pouch sets, one left and one right. (Each had five pouches and each pouch contained three chargers or 15 rounds of

munition. Total rounds 150.)
ne bayonet-frog.
ne water-bottle and carrier.
ne haversack.
ne valise or pack.
wo supporting straps for valise or pack.
ne entrenching tool with carriers for the head
d helve.

Northumberland Fusiliers after an attack at St Eloi, March 1916. Survivors for the time being, they are much happier to face the camera than the soldiers in the previous photograph. All wear the '08 pattern equipment with the haversack replacing the pack on the back. An unusual photograph: apart from the enemy souvenirs sported, there is a strange mixture of clean and muddy clothing and weapons. (Imperial War Museum)

assemble the equipment for Marching Order
e belt was first adjusted to suit the waist, the
yonet-frog was slid on, and the pouch sets were
ed to the belt front at left and right. Braces
ere then buckled to the pouch sets and passed
er the shoulders, crossing in the small of the
ck, and fastening to the buckles on the belt
ar. As the belt rear and each pouch set had a
n. strap passing downwards, there were now
ur strap-ends extending from below the pouch
ts and the belt rear for the attachment of other
ms. On the right side buckled the entrenching

tool head in its holder, with the water-bottle
buckled over it, and to the left side buckled the
haversack. To the rear of the bayonet-frog was a
strap to which the entrenching tool helve holder
buckled. When positioned this allowed the helve
to be carried on the side of the bayonet scabbard.
Finally, the valise or pack was buckled to two 'D'
buckles on the rear of the braces and to the
diagonal straps projecting from the pouch-sets.
This was the order of equipment in which the
British Expeditionary Force fought the opening
battles of the Great War in 1914.

Front view of '37 pattern Battle Order.

In the design stage the main item intended to be carried in the pack was the greatcoat. The haversack was for rations and similar necessaries, but it is clear from Regimental Orders of the time that much more was ordered to be carried in Marching Order. This, of course, had the effect of negating the aim of keeping the infantryman's total load to about 45lb. When the course of the Great War dictated the need for shrapnel helmets, respirators and grenades the burden of the infantryman rose to half the average man's body weight, or 75lb. The 1908 web equipment coped with this increased load, but it became clear that a new order was needed in which to fight. Therefore it became practice to dump packs at a convenient spot in rear of the front line, and by attaching the haversack to the braces in the manner of a small pack 'battle order' was borne.

Often it was necessary to attach the mess-tin [by] its handle to the flap straps of the haversack [in] order to create more space for the extra item[s] which now had to be carried in the haversac[k]. Even so, with extra ammunition, rations, and [so] forth the weight carried was considerable, an[d] marches in full equipment were limited to five [to] seven miles per day.

When infantry went into the attack in th[e] Great War only the first waves might expect [to] carry no more than Battle Order. Succeedin[g] waves were encumbered with wire, picket[s,] digging tools, extra ammunition and all the man[y] other items considered essential to the success [of] the attack and the subsequent consolidation [of] the objective. In these cases methods of carryin[g] the extras had to be improvised, and the le[ss] bulky items were tied to the equipment in san[d] bags or buckled to convenient parts of th[e] equipment.

Shortly after the introduction of the 190[8] pattern the need for equipment for soldiers arme[d] with the pistol became apparent. A leath[er] holster and pouch were introduced, with brac[e] attachments, to take the place of the pouch se[t] as attachment points for the braces and pac[k]. Other specialized webbing was introduce[d] during the Great War, notably carriers for Lew[is] gun magazines, tools and spares. These item[s] were made in webbing by the Mills Equipme[nt] Company, and were supplementary items to th[e] equipment.

The only modification to the 1908 pattern we[b] equipment was made in the early months of th[e] Great War, when it was found that ammunitio[n] was being lost from the left-hand pouches whe[n] the wearers leant against trench parapets in th[e] firing position, as pouch flaps were unsnapped b[y] contact with the breastworks. A strap and stu[d] fastening was designed for the three lower le[ft] pouches, and the modification was incorporate[d] into future items manufactured.

The 1908 pattern web infantry equipment wa[s] based on a sound design, flexible enough to en[-] compass the tactical changes forced upon th[e] infantry in the years of the 1914–18 War. That [it] soldiered on for 30 years until supplanted by a[n] equipment designed to carry light machine gu[n] magazines is a testament to its worth.

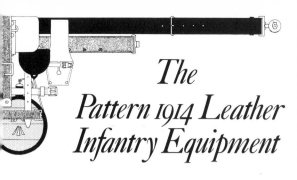

The Pattern 1914 Leather Infantry Equipment

Historical

The outbreak of war in August 1914 found the Mills Equipment Company unable immediately to supply the hundreds of thousands of sets of the 1908 pattern needed to equip the 'Kitchener's Armies' forming in the UK. Having equipped the standing armies of Britain and most of the Empire with the 1908 pattern equipment prior to the war, the Mills factories had virtually closed down. Now, with the need to expand and get into production on a scale never before envisaged, it would be some time before the company could meet demands.

A stop-gap was needed, and the answer was found in a pattern of leather equipment which followed the Mills-Burrowes design as closely as possible. The webbing haversack and pack of the 1908 pattern equipment were used, but with leather straps. The unique cartridge carriers of the Mills-Burrowes design, with their diagonal strap for load transference, proved impossible to copy in leather. A pouch similar to the patterns of earlier equipments was used, and the diagonal strap was transferred to the back of the waistbelt. Thus, with the first principle of the Mills-Burrowes design neglected, the weight of the pack bore directly down on the rear of the hips. Nevertheless, at a time when stocks of the 1903 bandolier equipment were being pressed into service, the new leather equipment seemed a very acceptable alternative until enough sets of the 1908 pattern became available.

Orders for a million sets of the pattern 1914 leather infantry equipment were placed with manufacturers of leather goods in Britain and the United States and, despite the original intention of using the equipment for training purposes only, it was not long before troops were using it in all theatres of war. As a general rule battalions equipped with the pattern 1914 leather equipment were re-equipped with the 1908 pattern for the Western Front up to 1916, but after this period the leather equipment was retained by the new battalions moving to France. Although evidence exists that both 1908 and 1914 equipment was worn within units this practice was rare, and generally a uniformity was maintained, at least at battalion level.

Description

Good quality brown leather was used in the manufacture of the pattern 1914 equipment, with a smooth texture for the belt and a grained finish for the other items. Stoutly sewn, the pouches, frogs, carriers and straps were reinforced with metal rivets to ensure maximum strength. Most of the metalwork was in brass, but parts of the belt-buckle were sometimes made of steel for extra strength.

The design of the pattern 1914 leather infantry equipment followed that of the 1908 pattern as

Rear view of '37 pattern Battle Order.

closely as possible except that the waistbelt and the ends of the braces were narrower and the pouches differed as already described. These were made to accommodate one cotton bandolier of 50 rounds each, so that a total of 100 rounds were carried as opposed to the 150 of the 1908 pattern.

The equipment was assembled in much the same manner as the 1908 pattern until it came to the fitting of the pack. Here there were no diagonal straps from the pouches to secure the bottom edge of the pack, therefore the two straps projecting from the rear of the waistbelt served in their stead. Balance of the pack was obtained by pulling the base of the pack as close to the belt as possible. With the top of the pack secured to the upper part of the braces the full weight of the pack was thus borne by the waistbelt, with

predictable discomfort.

The leather tongue of the waistbelt could used for obtaining rapid expansion of the belt comfort or when slipping the equipment on ov a greatcoat. The snake clasp of the buckle w simply hooked into a slot cut in the tongue, th gaining an instant adjustment of three inches.

A pistol case and pistol ammunition pou were later provided for troops armed with t pistol, and with these came brace attachme similar to the 1908 pattern. These brace attac ments were also used by troops such as medic orderlies who carried no arms or ammunition.

Rushed into service as a stop-gap, the patte 1914 leather infantry equipment gave sterli service on all fronts in the Great War. It w doomed to become obsolete as soon as the w was over because of the material from which mo of the set was made, and because of the desi flaw which threw the weight of the pack total on the hips. Few examples of the 1914 patte survive to this day, but the items that do rema are a tribute to the quality of their manufactu The author has a 1914 pattern waistbelt 'beat into a ploughshare' after the Great War and us for the 60 years since. It is as serviceable today on the day it was made.

Right rear view of '37 pattern Battle Order.

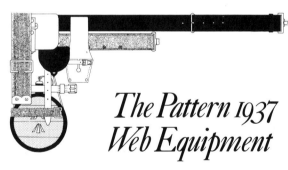

The Pattern 1937 Web Equipment

Historical

The Armistice of 1918 left the British Empi with enormous quantities of munitions. For t four years of war the factories had poured out an ever-increasing rate the armaments demand by the largest British Army ever put into the fiel Now, with the peace and the inevitable cutbac in manpower and money, the Regular Arm could look forward to nothing new until wartin ocks were expended. (The author's company was issued in 1970 with shell dressings manufactured and stored in 1917. Though an extreme example, this does illustrate the Army's approach to 'good housekeeping'.)

As far as infantry personal equipment was concerned, 1918 saw the British Army with large quantities of a design of web equipment which was only 10 years old and which had served well in the recent war. The 1914 leather equipment was phased out of service, and, against the background of hard times at home and abroad, the army went back to its peacetime job of policing the Empire wearing the '08 pattern equipment. In the years that followed cries for the expenditure of hard cash on costly military novelties fell upon deaf ears in the Treasury, until at last the ambitions of Hitler and his new Germany could no longer be ignored. In the late 1930s, with another world war looming, the re-arming and re-equipping of the Army to a standard sufficient to enable it to fight a 'mechanized' war was put in hand. In an eleventh-hour atmosphere some of the weapons and equipment needed to replace Great War items or to meet new tactical requirements were ordered into production. In the infantry sphere some items, notably the Bren light machine gun, were good designs suited to the tactical doctrine of the time; but it was inevitable that bad or obsolescent designs would be rushed into production in an atmosphere that allowed little time for the evaluation of badly-needed new items. It was at this time that the 1937 pattern web equipment was accepted as a replacement for the 1908 pattern, and indeed, as a personal equipment suitable for all arms of the Army in its new mechanized rôle. (Prior to the introduction of the 1937 equipment all troops in horsed units had a special-to-rôle set of personal equipment. The fledgling Tank Corps, originating from the infantry via the Machine Gun Corps, used the pistol-armed set of the 1908 pattern equipment. The 1937 pattern design was the first attempt to provide a set of equipment which, when suitably adapted, would serve the newly mechanized infantryman, gunner, tankman and sapper, in fact all but those still involved with horses— which the British military establishment still required in large numbers at the time.)

Development of infantry personal equipment in the inter-war years was a low-key affair, with design stemming mainly from the Mills Equipment Company acting on the authority of the War Office, who 'invited' the company to produce experimental sets for trials based on specifications supplied by the usual military committee. Military planners predicted that future wars would be wars of mobility rather than the static, slogging matches of 1914–18 and, in the early 1930s the Braithewaite Committee on the dress and equipment of the infantry soldier requested the Mills Equipment Company to design a set of personal equipment more suited to the needs of 'mobile war' than the 1908 pattern. Less ammunition need be carried on the man, it was considered; the equipment set itself should be lighter in weight, with no items hanging below

Front view of '37 pattern officer's set.

15

Rear view of '37 pattern officer's set.

the waistline. (The water-bottle was to be carried in a 'rucksack' pack, with access to it gained by slipping the pack off. It will be remembered that this could not be done with the 1908 pattern, which was a one-piece set when assembled.) It was envisaged that the pack or valise would be carried in unit transport. Four designs to these specifications were produced by the Mills Equipment Company, of which one set, the No. 3 design, was selected for a two-battalion trial in the UK.

Although the No. 3 design was accepted in principle as a suitable replacement for the 1908 equipment, progress on it came to a halt pending the evaluation of a new section light automatic weapon, the Bren. In 1936, with the Bren LMG accepted as a replacement for the Lewis gun, the Mills Equipment Company were asked to redesign their No. 3 set to accommodate its magazines.

Whether or not it was at this time that the decision was taken to change what had been an infantry equipment set into an all-arms equipment set is not clear, but it is quite clear that the No. 3 design began life as an infantry set, and equally clear that the 1937 pattern set that developed from it was designed as a universal equipment. The involvement of the Braithewaite Committee as regards its original charter is unclear from this point.

The Mills No. 3 design had a number of unique features. The cartridge belt was a belt in name only, being two cartridge carriers fastened at the front with a quick-release buckle and at the back by an adjustable strap. The rucksack, judging from available photographs, hung from the shoulders in the manner of the familiar hiker's item, and had two straps on the flap for a pick or shovel to be carried diagonally (a sensible idea which enabled the soldier to sit without mishap and to adopt a firing position without tipping his helmet over his eyes). The bayonet still hung well below the waist, but as the No. 4 rifle with its short cruciform bayonet was already scheduled to replace the No. 1 SMLE this was a problem that time and the issue of the No. 4 would solve.

Sound though the Mills No. 3 design was, the extensive modifications now called for resulted in a new design which resembled the No. 3 in none but the most trivial details. The determination of the War Office to have a separate waistbelt which could be used for 'walking out' is worth noting. The new design, eventually to be sealed as the 1937 pattern, underwent what are described as extensive trials, resulting in the first orders being placed with the Mills Equipment Company in 1938, the year of Munich. Thus, after a gestation period of six years, the 1937 pattern web equipment was born. It would serve—with its tropical modification, the 1944 pattern—for over twenty years before post-war defence budgets would permit its replacement. A compromise intended to serve several purposes, it developed from an unhappy period of 'stop-go', being finally rushed into production in the year's breathing space that Munich bought. It was not one of the best designs of equipment, but, considering the circumstances leading up to its acceptance, it would have been remarkable if it had been.

escription

he 1937 pattern web equipment was manu-
ctured from the same material, woven cotton
ebbing, as the set it replaced, the 1908 pattern.
 was waterproofed and dyed to a light khaki
lour. The metal fittings were made of brass, and
ost of the buckles were of the 'D' or tongueless
onfiguration which allowed quick release and
ljustment.

The central item of the equipment was the
aistbelt, the only item common to all sets and
·ders. Issued in three sizes to fit all girths it was
 in. wide and had a patent clasp buckle, the two
lves of which were positioned by runners or
des. The ends of the belt had metal tags with
oks which fastened into loops woven inside the
elt and with which the belt was adjusted. At the
ar of the belt were two buckles to which
stened the braces. These were made in two
ngths (47in. and 55in.) and had a 2in.-wide
rtion in the centre for the shoulders. One of the
aces had a loop sewn in so that the braces could
 fastened where they crossed between the
earer's shoulder-blades.

Infantry carried their ammunition in pairs of
sic pouches. These were rectangular items
ade to contain two Bren LMG magazines, or
enades, or bandoliers of small arms ammu-
tion. The flap fastened with a patent brass snap
stener (a tongue fastener in later patterns) and
 the top rear of each pouch was a buckle to
cure the front end of the braces. Above these
ickles were loops to which were attached the
oks of the shoulder-straps. The pouches were
cured to the belt by means of hooks. Non-
fantry troops carried the ammunition for their
les in cartridge carriers, although evidence
ists that infantry personnel were sometimes
ued with these items. Cartridge carriers were
irs of double pockets with each pocket contain-
g two chargers of ammunition, giving a total of
 rounds in a pair of cartridge carriers. The
rriers were fitted to the waistbelt by means of
oks, and had a buckle and loop arrangement
ove them identical to that of the basic pouch.

A frog was provided for the bayonet. As this
as somewhat less stable than the '08 pattern
g a loop for the handle of the SMLE bayonet
as provided in an attempt to reduce the oscilla-

Left front view of '37 pattern officer's set.

tion of the bayonet as the wearer moved.

Although the water-bottle, identical to the '08
pattern item, was intended to be carried in the
haversack in Battle Order, a carrier was provided
to enable it to be suspended from the ends of the
braces when Field Service Marching Order was
worn. There were two types of carrier. One was a
framework of web straps similar to the '08
pattern, and the other was made as a complete
pocket for the bottle.

The haversack, or small pack as it came to be
called, was a rectangular bag 11in. by 9in. by
4in., and was carried high on the back. It was
divided internally into three sections intended to
take the water-bottle and a new rectangular
pattern of mess-tin, with the groundsheet and
other necessary items in the main compartment.
Buckles and straps were attached to the haversack so that it could be worn either on the back

17

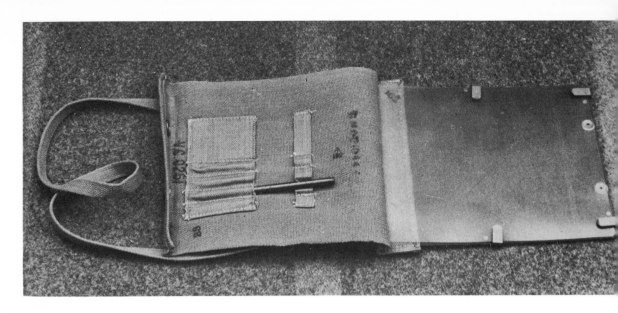

1937 pattern map case.

by means of shoulder-straps, or fastened to the brace-ends in Field Service Marching Order. The 'L'-shaped shoulder-straps were in pairs, left and right, consisting of a wide vertical and a narrow horizontal portion joined in the centre with a hook which could fasten to the pouch, brace attachment or cartridge carrier. The wide end of the shoulder-strap had a buckle for the tab of the haversack or valise, and the narrow end fastened to a buckle on the haversack or valise strap.

The brace attachments came in pairs and were intended for the use of personnel armed with pistols or not armed at all (Medical Corps, etc.). They enabled the braces to be fastened to the front of the belt in the absence of pouches or cartridge carriers, and provided anchorage points for the shoulder-straps.

Officers and troops armed with pistols (but not Royal Armoured Corps personnel armed with pistols) were issued with a pistol case and pistol ammunition pouch. The pistol case was designed to accommodate the .38in. No. 2 Pistol and would not accept other pistols gracefully, if at all. It was intended to be fastened to the waistbelt by means of hooks, and had a similar hook to connect to the ammunition pouch when this was worn above it. In this way the pistol case was often suspended

below the belt hanging from the pouch. The pistol ammunition pouch was identical to the compass pocket except that the latter was lined with felt to protect the compass.

Binoculars were carried in a case also lined with felt, but with the additional protection of a vulcanite box immediately within the case. The binocular case could be attached to the waistbelt with metal hooks or slung from a brace or brace-ends.

Officers were issued with an additional item in the shape of the officer's haversack. This was a briefcase-like item measuring 12in. by 9in. by 2in.; it could be suspended from the brace-ends or carried loose by means of a handle on the flap. The interior was divided in two and had additional compartments for pencils, protractors and dividers. The carrying capacity of the officer's haversack was considerably less than the normal haversack, and it was intended for maps, notebooks and other small items only.

The valise or pack, called the 'large pack' to distinguish it from the haversack or 'small pack' was retained from the '08 pattern equipment with its valise or supporting straps. Worn only in Marching Order, as when changing stations, etc., it was usually carried in unit transport when in action.

The equipment was assembled according to the set and the order required. The sets were:

(1)   Set for infantry (basic pouches).

2) Set with cartridge carriers (non-infantry).

3) Set for personnel armed with pistols (pistol case and ammo pouch).

4) Set for officers (as for 3, but with binocular and compass case and officer's haversack).

The orders were:

1) Field Service Marching Order (valise worn on back, haversack and water-bottle suspended from the brace ends).

2) Battle Order (haversack worn on back with the water-bottle inside).

3) Skeleton or Musketry Order (as for Battle Order less haversack).

4) Drill Order (belt and sidearms only).

To assemble any form of set the belt was first adjusted to fit, the bayonet-frog was slid on to the left side, and either the basic pouches, cartridge carriers or brace attachments were positioned either side of the belt-buckle at the front of the belt. The braces were then attached to the pouches, carriers or attachments, taking care to mesh the braces where they crossed in the rear of the body, and then buckled to the rear of the belt. Personnel armed with the pistol then fitted the pistol case to the belt on the left side and the pistol ammo pouch on the right. (Officers fitted the binocular case on the right side with the pistol ammo pouch and the compass pocket above the pistol case and binocular case respectively.) With the belt, braces and pouch, etc. combination assembled and put on, there only remained the attachment and adjustment of the shoulder-straps to the haversack, and it too could be put on to form Battle Order.

Although it was originally intended that no item should hang down from the belt in Battle Order, it was soon necessary to resort to this expedient in order to accommodate the entrenching tools which were introduced in the early years of the war, and to carry the water-bottle in its carrier in order to make room in the haversack for the extra items considered vital to the soldier in battle by the promulgators of Regimental Standing Orders. In the latter case it had been considered sufficient when designing the haversack to make it large enough to accommodate only a water-bottle, mess-tin (containing rations), knife, fork and spoon, pullover and groundsheet. Making room for towel, soap, razor, boot-brush, dubbin, etc. ousted the water-bottle, negating the aims of the originator of the specification and the designer, and condemning the infantryman to an item that flapped and bounced as he ran. As it took almost four years of war before the No. 4

Detail of '37 pattern basic pouches, brace attachment, waistbelt and brace.

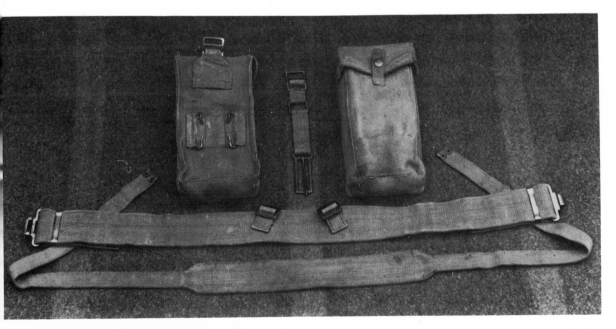

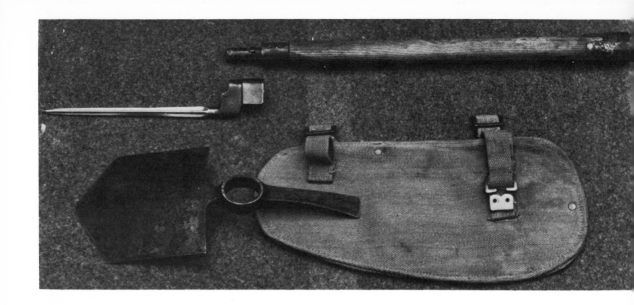

Detail of '37 pattern entrenching tool and holder. The No. 4 bayonet is shown, to indicate the adaptation of the helve as a 'mine-prodder'.

rifle began to replace the SMLE, the long sword-bayonet flapped on the side opposite the water-bottle, whilst at the rear of the belt an entrenching tool hung and also flapped and bounced.

There were two types of entrenching tool. The first pattern was similar to the German Army item, but this was rejected in favour of a reversion to the mattock-style tool of the Great War. A modification to allow the spike-bayonet of the No. 4 rifle to be fitted to the helve of this second pattern of entrenching tool created a useful mine-prodder; but with a helmet, a respirator and a gas cape rolled and tied above the haversack, the infantryman of 1942 now carried slightly more than his counterpart of 1918.

Fitting the 1937 pattern equipment to obtain some degree of comfort was never an easy task, and was sometimes impossible. The waistbelt had to be worn as tight as possible if it was not to be drawn up under the ribs at the front by the weight of the haversack. The haversack itself only rode comfortably if drawn up at the back of the neck. In this position it, and the cape tied above it, constantly tipped the helmet over the eyes, while the shoulder-straps, where they passed under the arms, cut into the armpits and restricted the circulation. If worn 'rucksack'

style, low on the back, the haversack leapt up an down when the wearer ran, striking him re peatedly on the back of the head. Finding compromise that would ensure reasonable com fort was possible for a large, well-built soldier bu was virtually impossible for a smaller man.

Most ex-soldiers who used the 1937 patter equipment will probably remember it best fo the numberless hours spent blancoing its strap pouches and packs and polishing the dozens c brass buckles, tags and fasteners. For thei amusement I feel compelled to quote part of th chapter headed 'Care and Preservation of th Equipment' in the official 1939 pamphlet describ ing the 1937 pattern equipment. This states Should the equipment become in a dirty c greasy condition, it may be washed, using warr water, soap and a sponge . . . The metal wor will not be polished, but allowed to get dull, s as to avoid catching the rays of the sun.'

In addition to personal equipment man supplementary items were manufactured i webbing for the infantry. Noteworthy are th utility pouch sets for the carriage of LMG maga zines, anti-tank rifle magazines, 2in. morta ammunition, etc.; the holdalls, special sling and spare parts wallets for the Bren LMG; an the special pouch sets for Thompson SMG an automatic pistol magazines. All these items coul be found within the infantry platoon. Ther were many other webbing carriers and cases fo infantry signals equipment, etc., but these ar rguably outside the scope of this book.

The 1937 pattern equipment was at best dequate for the job it had to do. That the quipment which replaced it after long and xtensive research and development was excel- ent by comparison was in large part due to the hortcomings of the 1937 design.

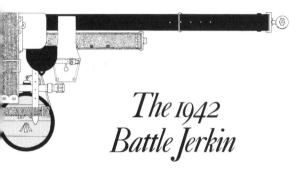

The 1942 Battle Jerkin

Dissatisfaction with the 1937 pattern web equip- ment and its limitations in the opening battles nd campaigns of the Second World War gave vay, in military circles, to a school of belief that vebbing had seen its day as a personal load- arrying equipment for the infantryman. The 937 equipment was hard to modify to adapt to ew tactical thinking, although crude attempts o solve the problem of the dangling sword- ayonet led to the frog being fixed to the left houlder-strap of the haversack so that the bayonet was carried in the contemporary American manner. Carriage of a pick or shovel was effected by slipping the implement between the wearer's back and the haversack, or attach- ing it between the flap-straps of the haversack with a piece of wood. Whatever the shortcomings of the 1937 pattern, it was hard to envisage a replacement for it in the middle of a world war; nevertheless, in 1942 the Chief Ordnance Officer of the Field Stores, Aldershot—Colonel E. R. Rivers-Macpherson—devised an infantry equipment that was a complete departure from the equipment design and evolution of the past 300 years.

Colonel Rivers-Macpherson had a low opinion of the 1937 pattern equipment. In his pamphlet introducing his Battle Jerkin he claimed that most infantry COs regarded the 1937 equipment as clumsy, noisy, restricting of mobility, difficult to get through obstacles, allowing no flexibility for weapons, cramping, uncomfortable and galling to the soldier! He further considered the 1937 pattern equipment to be no advance on that worn 100 years previously. After a careful summary of what a modern equipment ought to afford, the Colonel introduced his answer to the problem, which he described as 'a simple and

Detail of '37 pattern pistol case, binocular case, and frog for wire-cutters.

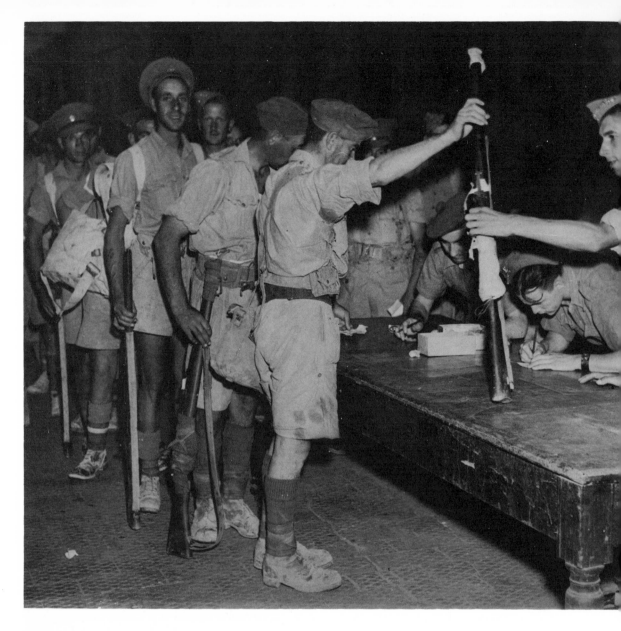

8th Army men hand in rifles at a Cairo leave centre in 1942. Note the '37 pattern cartridge carriers, the Bombay bloomers worn by the nearest man and the general appearance of men just off the desert. *(Soldier Magazine)*

easy-fitting garment, on the lines of a poacher's jacket'. The item was to be called a battle jerkin.

The battle jerkin was made of chocolate brown cotton duck material and was waterproofed. It resembled a hip-length waistcoat with a multitude of exterior and interior pockets. Made in three sizes to suit all average shapes of infantry figure, it weighed $2\frac{3}{4}$lb against the full $5\frac{1}{2}$lb of the conventional '37 pattern battle order.

The jerkin could accommodate a phenomenal amount of kit. The universal pockets on the chest could each hold two Bren mags, or one pair of wire-cutters, or one Boys anti-tank rifle magazine, or six Thompson magazines, or five Sten magazines, or 100 rounds of small arms ammo, or six grenades, or one signal pistol, or a pair of binoculars, or a pistol with its ammunition. The right bomb pocket could hold four grenades, or two 2in. mortar bombs, or two slabs of gun-cotton. The left bomb pocket could hold the water-bottle, or six grenades, or two 2in. mortar bombs, or three slabs of gun-cotton.

The No. 4 bayonet was carried in the leading edge of the left bomb pocket, and a commando knife or SMLE bayonet could be carried in a pocket on the left lower chest. An inside pocket in the 'tail' of the jerkin was intended for soft items, while an outside pocket in the same region accepted the entrenching tool head or two 2in. mortar bombs. The pack pocket was capable of carrying the gas cape, 48 hours' rations, knife, fork and spoon, iron ration, mess-tin and 100 rounds of small arms ammunition. On either side of the pack pocket were frogs for the entrenching tool helve and a machete in its sheath. The jerkin had a further inside pocket in the chest region for maps, a tab to secure a pistol holster, and ventilating panels in the waist, while each pocket had a drain hole to permit rapid drainage should the wearer have to swim. On the shoulders were whipcord loops to secure items carried on the back, and stops to prevent slings, etc. slipping from the shoulders. Two buckles fitting at the waist and lower chest secured the jerkin, and either form of respirator then in service could be worn beneath it.

Colonel Rivers-Macpherson made many claims on behalf of his invention, including:

1) Accessibility of weapons and ammunition, coupled with flexibility of variety of the same.
2) Easy to put on and take off.
3) A Mae West could be worn beneath the jerkin and could be inflated and used in that position.
4) The jerkin was absolutely silent.
5) It gave protection from rain.
6) Its camouflage qualities were better than webbing.
7) It was much more comfortable to wear than webbing.

In August 1942 a trial to compare the battle jerkin with the '37 pattern web equipment was conducted by the RAMC. Results showed marginally in favour of the jerkin, despite claims that it made a soldier hotter on the march than did webbing.

From this moment on the fortunes of the battle jerkin declined, as might have even the most revolutionary design in the face of massive wartime production and issue of the 1937 pattern web equipment. Made in small numbers, the battle jerkin first saw action on the beaches of Normandy on D-Day, used by some of the commandos and assault infantry. From June 1944 it seems to have disappeared into obscurity, suffering its final indignity by being sold off in the days of post-war shortages as a garment 'useful to hikers'. It never again saw service in any military context, although it would—in a modified form—be used as a contender in the trials of the 1950s to find a replacement for the 1937 web equipment. Readers may wonder why such a revolutionary and obviously useful item suffered such a fate. In the opinion of the author it had one enormous disadvantage. To the eyes of the Colonel Blimps of the time it appeared scruffy and unmilitary. It had no 'waistbelt for walking out', and only two brass buckles that could be polished!

Infantry officer demonstrating the equipment of the infantryman to RAF officers at the Middle East Combined Operations Training Centre, November 1943. Note the method of carrying packs and shovels in '37 pattern equipment. Also visible are 'respirators, anti-gas, light', and a 1in. signal pistol in its leather case. (Imperial War Museum)

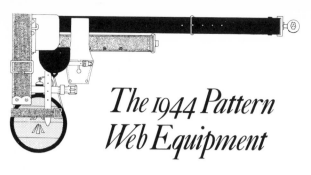

The 1944 Pattern Web Equipment

Historical

The entry of the Japanese into the Second World War found the Allies ill-prepared to fight a campaign in the conditions prevailing in the Far East. Japanese successes following the Pearl Harbor attack were due as much to the inability of the Allies to adapt tactically to terrain and climate as to any other factor.

With military priorities, thinking and doctrine geared to the European theatre of operations, much time was to pass before the British were able to cope with the difficulties confronting them in Burma and to get on with the task of regaining territory lost to the Japanese in early 1942. Operations such as the first Chindit expedition in 1943 highlighted the need for formations to be able to operate without the traditionally accepted forms of lines of communications and transport, and discovered shortcomings in some of the standard weaponry and equipment.

At this time planning staffs were preparing for a long and arduous campaign to defeat Japanese land forces in the territories they had conquered and in the home islands of Japan itself. The atomic bomb and the way in which it would abruptly end the war in the Far East were unknown to these planners, who considered it might take until 1947 to force Japan into unconditional surrender. Therefore consideration was given to special-to-theatre weapons and equipment to aid Allied ground forces in the difficult task they faced.

One of the decisions taken as a result of the Lethbridge Mission to the Far East in 1944 was that the 1937 pattern web equipment should be modified to produce a design more suited to the needs of the infantryman in the light of recent experience. The equipment called for was to be similar to the 1937 pattern but with webbing which was lighter, thinner and more pliable. The shoulder-straps were to be wider, and an aluminium water-bottle was called for.

A pattern of equipment based on these specifications was produced by the Mills Equipment Company and was considered by the British military authorities as well as another pattern of jungle equipment being developed by the company at the time. After much modification a set of equipment based on the best features of both designs finally emerged and was sealed as the 1944 pattern web equipment.

Production and issue of the 1944 pattern was such that it did not see service during the Second World War. The atomic bombing of Hiroshima and Nagasaki and the unconditional surrender of Japan removed the need for the new equipment on any large scale, as was the case with many other Far East items under development or production at the time. However, British airborne units engaged in aiding the Dutch in the civil war which followed the Allied re-occupation of Java in late 1945 used the 1944 pattern equipment in combat.

Airborne and parachute formations became the first and the only exclusive users of the 1944 pattern equipment in the post-war years, and continued to use it until it was replaced by the 1958 pattern equipment. Otherwise the '44 pattern, as it came to be called, became a theatre issue used for the purpose for which it was designed: campaigning in the Far East. British and Commonwealth troops used the '44 pattern in the Korean War, the Malayan 'Emergency', the operations against Mau-Mau in Kenya, and in other minor wars east of Suez. The equipment still soldiers on to this day with only one official modification—the moving of the pouches to a position similar to that of the '58 pattern.

The advantages of the 1944 pattern equipment when compared to the equipment it was designed to replace for Far East campaigning, the '37 pattern, were not outstanding. That it was less durable than the '37 pattern is beyond dispute; the webbing frayed and split more readily, and the metal alloy fitments fractured and slipped

The Pattern 1908 Web Infantry Equipment

A

The Pattern 1914 Leather Infantry Equipment

B

The Pattern 1937 Web Equipment

C

The Pattern 1937 Web Equipment

D

The 1942 Battle Jerkin

1

The 1944 Pattern Web Equipment

2

3

4

5

6

7

F

The 1958 Pattern Web Equipment

G

Future Developments

...der great weight or stress. In Malaya, where ...avy loads had to be carried by the infantryman ...some of the worst conditions of terrain and ...mate in the world, drastic modification of the ...4 pattern equipment was necessary, with all ...t the haversack and water-bottle being dis-...rded in favour of improvised belts, pouches and ...ck straps. In some cases the '37 pattern pack ...as preferred to the '44 pattern haversack. Con-...dering that the '44 equipment was specifically ...signed for jungle use it was disappointing to ...d that it fell short of operational requirements ...the Malayan war, where the ammunition, food ...d necessaries carried by the infantry patrols ...re cut to the bare necessities. (Even so a Bren ...nner in Malaya would be carrying 85lb at the ...tset of an operation. The weight would de-...ease slightly as he consumed the four days' ...od he carried. The weight would be resupplied ...the next airdrop!)

The '44 pattern equipment was probably at ...best when carrying normal loads for which the ...versack was well adapted. The water-bottle, ...th its useful cup and accessible cover, was ...obably the best item of the equipment. The ...uipment found most favour with the soldier of ...e immediate post-war years in that it could not ...blancoed and had no brass to polish—a not ...considerable boon at the time.

escription

...he set was made of lightweight webbing dyed ...ngle-green and proofed against rot. The metal ...tings were made of lightweight anodized alloy. ...he waistbelt was of the back-adjusting type, ...ing made in three sections, the left and right ...ctions having a patent buckle attached and a ...asp for the braces. A webbing loop to fasten ...e butt of the rifle when carried slung was sewn ...the right section. The centre or back portion ...the belt had buckles for the braces, and a ...w of eyelets to secure the water-bottle carrier, ...achete sheath, etc. were inserted at two-inch ...tervals along the entire lower edge of the belt. ...Following specifications, the pouches were ...uch larger than the '37 pattern type. Otherwise ...ey were manufactured in the same style as the ...7 pattern, except that the left-hand pouch had ...ops on one side to hold a short bayonet. A

separate bayonet-frog was also issued for longer bayonets.

The braces had wide (3in.) shoulder sections tapering to 1in. straps at the front and pairs of 1in. straps at the rear. These rear straps were joined together to make the braces a one-piece set. The braces attached to the pouches (or brace attachments) at the front of the wearer and crossed at the back of the wearer to attach to the belt-buckles and clasps. This configuration was designed for two purposes. It was considered to give more stability to the increased weight in the pouches; and the belt centre or back section could be removed to allow a soldier with a rash or sore in the waist area to wear the equipment without undue discomfort. To the belt fastened the water-bottle carrier by means of a wire clip which engaged in the eyelets of the belt. The machete sheath attached to the belt in the same manner.

The haversack had a waterproof central main compartment with two pockets on either side large enough to take the mess-tin halves. The poncho or groundsheet was rolled and secured below the haversack by means of two straps. There was provision for the attachment of a pick or shovel, or an entrenching tool, by means of straps on the flap and body of the haversack. Shoulder-straps similar to the '37 pattern variety secured the haversack in position, and these clipped to the buckle on top of the pouch. A strap passed from the bottom edge of the haver-sack around the lower chest, passing through loops on the inside upper edges of the pouches. (Whatever the intended purpose of this strap, it was nearly always used as a supplementary strap for the attachment of the poncho.)

A rucksack was designed for use with the '44 pattern equipment. It was intended to be worn either from the shoulder-straps in the manner of a pack (in which case the haversack was worn suspended from the brace-ends on the left side) or fastened to a manpack frame. These rucksacks were seldom issued and extremely hard to come by. They were an excellent item, and the author was lucky enough to acquire one which he used in Malaya until it fell to pieces; it was sadly missed.

Also issued with the '44 pattern equipment

were pistol holsters, brace attachments, binocular cases and pistol ammunition/compass cases for the officer's set or for those soldiers armed with the pistol.

The 1958 Pattern Web Equipment

Historical

The victory of 1945 saw a situation similar to that of 1918. The huge industrial potential of Great Britain had been geared for six years to the task of winning the production race that would decide the outcome of the war. Now, war-weary and bankrupt, the nation surveyed the vast parks and dumps of military stores that the peace had made surplus to requirements.

Amongst the redundant implements of war there were huge quantities of the 1937 pattern web equipment. Available, too, were the orders of the special-to-theatre 1944 pattern web equipment which the early surrender of Japan had prevented from seeing service. With these stocks on hand, and money available for nothing but the barest military essentials, it was predictable that the 1937 and 1944 patterns, imperfect though they were, would have to serve the British Army for some time to come.

It was not until 1950 that the War Office decided to go ahead with the development of an improved design of load-carrying equipment, and the following year saw the appearance of the Ordnance-designed 1951 experimental web equipment—Z2 pattern—which underwent evaluation in competition with current equipments, modified and unmodified. Testing and development was a lengthy and unhurried business from here on—probably as a result of

the experience of the unfortunate sequence events which led to the acceptance of the 19. pattern equipment—with the War Office d termined to get it right this time. It was not un 1956 that serving soldiers got their first glimp of the shape of things to come, as the equipme. that would eventually become the 1958 patte began to appear for large-scale troop trials.

At about this time designers of military loa carrying equipment world-wide were beginni to arrive at similar conclusions. Almost as if th had got together to talk it all over they agre that the best solution was to start with a padd yoke over the shoulders from which braces suspenders attached front and rear to a wai belt. With a pair of pouches large enough to ta two rifle magazines, a canteen, entrenching to and a small valise fixed to the sides and rear the belt, they were in business. What had be the problem all these years? Thus the America and the British contrived to produce sets of pe sonal equipment remarkably alike, with th armies of the nations under their influen following their lead, and most others eventua following suit. (A study of the infantry person equipment used on both sides of the Iron Curta today is most enlightening. Very few designs fa to conform to the yoke-and-belt concept. On the Chinese, with their bib-and-brace equip ment, seem to be the odd men out.)

In Great Britain the re-equipping of th infantry with the 1958 pattern web equipme was well under way by 1960. With little regr battalions handed in their 1937 pattern webbin NAAFI sales of blanco and metal polish slumpe alarmingly, and serving infantrymen enjoyed f the first time a set of personal equipment th had been carefully thought out, was reasonab comfortable to wear, and had provision for mo needs in battle.

Description

The 1958 pattern web equipment is still in se vice with the British Army today; it is mac

Fine study of a corporal piper of the Queen's Own Camer Highlanders, North Africa 1942. Note the '37 pattern pist set. (*Soldier Magazine*)

26

om woven cotton webbing, pre-shrunk and ~~dy~~ed dark green. The main feature of the equip~~m~~ent is the yoke, which spreads the weight to be ~~b~~orne over the shoulders. The yoke consists of ~~t~~wo broad padded shoulder pieces joined in the ~~ar~~ea of the shoulder-blades by a lateral piece to ~~w~~hich is stitched a strap-and-buckle device for ~~at~~taching the lightweight pick or shovel. At either ~~si~~de of the lateral piece adjustable straps are ~~st~~itched, each of which attaches to the waistbelt ~~re~~ar by means of pads and hooks. At the front ~~ex~~tremities of the yoke are stitched quick-release ~~b~~uckles and long straps; these latter pass through ~~lo~~ops on the pouch, pistol-case or binocular case ~~a~~t the front of the waistbelt and are secured back ~~t~~o the quick-release buckle. (By means of this ~~st~~rap-and-buckle arrangement rapid adjustment ~~o~~f the tension between belt and yoke can be ~~m~~ade, thus shifting weight from the shoulders to ~~th~~e waist. This can be quite a boon on the ~~m~~arch.) To complete the yoke, loops are stitched ~~t~~o the shoulder pieces to secure the straps of the ~~fi~~eld pack, a webbing loop in rear and a metal ~~lo~~op in front.

The waistbelt is similar to the '37 pattern as ~~re~~gards size and the buckle/runner arrangement, ~~b~~ut the buckles, like all metal parts on the equip~~m~~ent, are made of steel or alloy and finished in ~~g~~reen or black. Adjustment of the belt is obtained ~~w~~ith hooks and a series of eyelets running along ~~th~~e belt's centre. Stitched to the rear of the belt ~~a~~re two metal loops for the attachment of the ~~c~~ape carrier.

The ammunition pouches, which are fastened ~~to~~ the belt by hooks, come as a set, left and right. ~~T~~he pouches hold a variety of combinations of ~~a~~mmunition and magazines, while the left pouch ~~h~~as a bayonet-frog on its side, and the right ~~p~~ouch has a pocket originally intended for the ~~n~~ow-obsolescent rifle-grenade launcher. (It ~~m~~akes a convenient spot to stow a knife, fork and ~~sp~~oon set.) Both pouches have a metal loop on ~~th~~eir rear-facing side for the attachment of the

cape carrier. The present pattern of pouch is much larger than the first pattern issued; this enlargement, with the web loops on the shoulder pads of the yoke, are the only major modifications to the set since its issue.

Fastened to the belt at the rear are a connected pair of large ('kidney') pouches for the carriage of mess-tins, water-bottle (before the issue of the current pattern the '08/'37 variety was used), rations, etc. The method of attachment is a complicated affair designed so that the large pouch set can be released by pulling a number of tags (two on the first sets, four at present). This quick-release device was built in to enable the wearer to rid himself of the burden of the kidney pouches without having to take the whole set off, and is a throwback to the 'drop your packs before battle' school of thought. The kidney pouches themselves are simple rectangular affairs with a white name-tag stitched to the rear surface of one pouch, and a loop to contain a 'utility' strap (a

Front view of '44 pattern Battle Order.

29

Commandos at an assembly area in the south of England prior to embarkation for D-Day, June 1944. Most of the men in view are wearing the 1942 Battle Jerkin. Note also the lightweight airborne folding bicycles with Bergen rucksacks on the carriers. (Imperial War Museum)

simple strap and buckle) on the inside of the flap of both.

Below the kidney pouches is fastened a cape carrier. This connects to the belt and the ammunition pouches by means of four spring-loaded hooks. The carrier's purpose is to contain a groundsheet or poncho in such a way that it is accessible. In the experimental sets the cape carrier was a cage-like series of straps, but the issue carrier is a simple rectangle of web material into which the poncho is rolled. Two quick-release tabs with two adjustment positions fasten the carrier, while on its top surface there is a

container for the head of the lightweight pick and a securing strap for the helve of the pick or the shaft of the lightweight shovel.

Completing the set to form what is termed Combat Equipment, Fighting Order (CEFO) is a plastic water-bottle and mug combination in a webbing carrier which fits to the belt on one side of the kidney pouches.

Fitting of the 1958 pattern web equipment is not difficult nor such a critical task as on previous sets. A soldier could only ensure comfort with the '08 pattern, and some degree of comfort with the '37 pattern, if he adjusted the set exactly. Once fitted, the '08 and '37 pattern sets could only be re-adjusted by removing the whole set. One of the best features of the '58 pattern set is that it can be adjusted and re-adjusted while being worn. The belt need not be tight and a great variety of adjustment—and hence, relief from galling—can be obtained by lengthening or shortening the race-straps at the front of the body (vertical nsion) and the straps connecting the cape rrier to the ammunition pouches (lateral nsion).

Issued with the '58 pattern set are a lightweight ck or shovel. These are slightly cut-down rsions of the general service pick and shovel and e almost as efficient as the full-size item. They e carried on the equipment in the region of the ine, and are attached as already described.

As pistols had gone out of favour when the '58 ttern web equipment appeared (only two were ued to an infantry battalion) no provision was ade for their carriage in the set. Pistol cases of anadian manufacture, supplied with the owning 9mm automatic then coming into rvice, served for those officers occasionally seen ith pistols. However, the involvement of the ilitary in Northern Ireland brought about a quirement for pistols to be issued on a much rger scale, and a pistol case to fit the '58 pattern t was designed and issued. Shortly after this it as realized that the '37 pattern compass and nocular cases also fitted badly into the '58 ttern set, and new designs of these two items ere also issued.

The now-familiar dark green webbing used in e manufacture of the '58 equipment is also used make the various wallets and cases needed for e present generation of platoon weapons. The al item in the family of '58 pattern equipment the field pack. Although it can be worn— rched above the kidney pouches and fastened the loops on the braces and ammo pouches to rm Combat Equipment, Marching Order CEMO)—it is rarely used for any other purpose an the stowage of personal kit in unit transport.

The 1958 pattern web equipment is as good a sign of personal load-carrying equipment as ay in the world today. It is not perfect, but either is any known set. Only by the reduction the infantryman's load through the intro- iction of small-calibre weapons—with a re- iltant drop in weight of weapons and, more iportant, ammunition—can an equipment be und that comes somewhere near the perfect lution. In service for 20 years, the 1958 pattern eb equipment has almost reached the service an of the '37 pattern and the '08 pattern—21

Rear view of '44 pattern Battle Order.

Rear view of '44 pattern Battle Order, without pack.

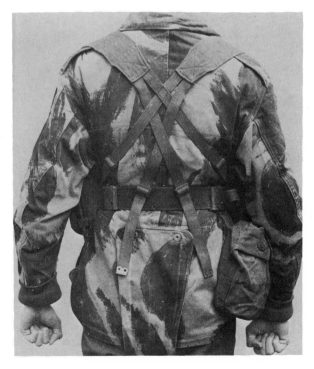

Right view of '44 pattern Battle Order.

Left view of '44 pattern Battle Order.

years each; but it seems unlikely that the curren set will be replaced by something new for som time yet.

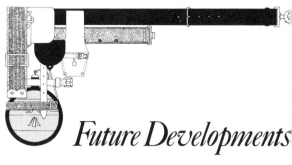

Future Developments

Like the current US and West German con figurations, the 1958 pattern equipment centre around a waistbelt to which are attached th pouches, etc., containing the combat load. yoke linked to the belt helps to spread some of th weight to the shoulders, but discomfort is ex perienced when the weight bears on the hips fo long periods. Despite this drawback no apparen effort has been made to design the waistbelt out the equipment sets undergoing development Judging by photographs published in the pres the experimental equipment is the mixture a before, looking remarkably similar to the 195 pattern and differing from it mainly in th material from which it is made. (Here a de parture from woven cotton webbing is contem plated in favour of nylon-butyl materials. On reason given for the change is that equipmen made from, or coated with, plastics can be de contaminated more easily after exposure to th effects of nuclear or chemical strikes.)

Other modifications appear to be in the size the ammunition pouches, which are larger tha those in current service; and the possible replace ment of the kidney pouches by an item similar t the 1937 pattern haversack or small pack which attached to the rear of the waistbelt. It sits on th buttocks and looks similar to the valise of 1871 i size, shape and location. Unfortunately th unique method of suspension of the 1871 valis has not been copied, and the new pack hang rom the belt in the manner condemned by the ommission which studied the Slade-Wallace quipment in 1903! The field pack is retained in vhat appears to be its original form, and, in an ttempt to solve the problems of the carriage of he lightweight digging tools, a folding shovel is under development. (One hopes that a reversion o an 'entrenching tool' is not being contemplated. Experience has repeatedly shown these to be unsuitable for getting underground quickly and with minimum expenditure of effort. Soldiers of the Second World War, knowing that their lives depended on getting under cover whenever they halted in range of enemy artillery or mortars, put up with the inconvenience of carrying a full-blown General Service shovel or pick. It is recorded that green troops had to be ordered to dig shell-scrapes. The veteran survivors of German 'stonks' needed no such urging. One company commander told me that he had, on occasions, fallen asleep digging. Even in a state of almost total exhaustion he knew he had to get underground to guarantee safety.)

Working on the principle that the replacement equipment set for the 1958 pattern should be an improvement on the best design the British infantry ever had, an excellent pattern should be in the offing. Whether or not this proves to be the case, the difficulties facing the agency responsible for the new design should not be underestimated. The team designing or modifying a set of personal

Current pattern British Army mess-tin with combination knife, fork and spoon set. This pattern was introduced into service with the '37 pattern web equipment. First issued in tin-plated pressed steel, the mess-tin is now made of aluminium.

equipment for infantry use must centre their design around the load the soldier must carry. This has been a difficult enough job in the past, but is even more complicated today when the range of weapons, ammunition and communications equipment carried within the infantry platoon is more complex than ever. Even so it would seem that with the advent of the 4.85mm Individual Weapon and the 4.85mm Section Weapon the problem of the carriage of ammunition in belts for the GPMG has been eliminated. (This was a vexed question and never properly

Detail of 1944 pattern pistol ammo pouch, water-bottle carrier, brace attachment and waistbelt.

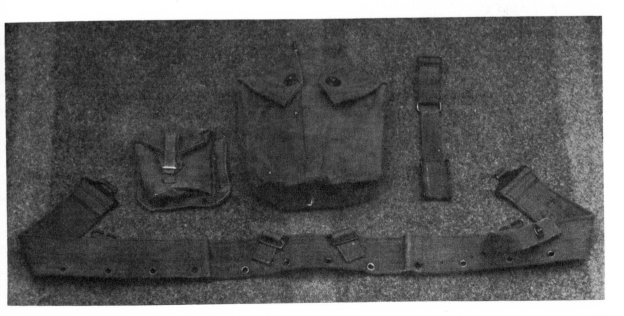

Front view, '58 pattern CEFO (Combat Equipment, Fighting Order).

Rear view, '58 pattern CEFO.

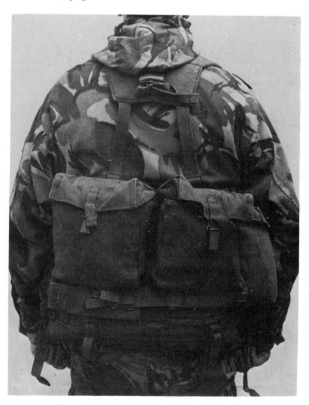

solved. The picture of riflemen camouflaged effectively but festooned with bandoliers of glittering belted ammunition posed an obvious problem. Ideas were advanced to dull the ammunition chemically, cover the belts with cotton sleeves, etc.; but apart from the camouflage aspect, belted ammo carried as bandoliers was liable to pick up grit and mud as the soldier moved about and cause stoppages when fired. The sensible thing to do was to stuff belted ammo into a pouch, but with a full scale of other kinds of ammunition there was often no room.) Small arms ammunition in magazines and bandoliers, plus grenades, would seem to be the ammunition load common to all infantrymen, but there remains the question of the carriage of ammunition for the two types of anti-tank weapon and the light mortar or its replacement. The man-packed radio is also vital to the modern infantryman and, used as they are in increasing numbers, personal equipment must be designed that will not impede the carriage of the present generation of back-packed radios. (Of course, lighter and more compact radios must be under development but —at the time of writing—have not come into service.)

Weapons, ammunition, radios, digging tools, NBC equipment and water: all these items must be considered when designing an infantry personal equipment set. It is arguable that these should be the only considerations and that extras such as rations, mess-tin and lightweight water-proofs should be carried in the pockets of the combat clothing. Operations requiring the carriage of extra rations, sleeping bags, etc. call for the provision of a rucksack-type pack to supplement basic equipment, but these types of operation are generally outside the scope of warfare in the European context. Here, at present, most infantry are APC-borne and rarely fight far from their steeds for protracted periods. Hence they need carry on their persons only those items essential to them in battle. Even so, as stressed before, this represents a substantial load.

One of the most interesting developments in the field of infantry personal equipment is a design accepted into service by the Finnish Army —an army with a creditable record in war and a reputation for excellence in design where in-

antry weapons and equipment are concerned. The Finns use a one-piece item which is more like a garment than a set of equipment in the traditional sense. It has little in common with the 1942 Battle Jerkin featured earlier, but reminds his writer of the angler's waistcoat or 'skeet jacket' seen in catalogues of sporting clothing. There is no waistbelt at all. The pouches hanging diagonally from the region of the lower chest and outwards towards the hips are supported at their upper and lower corners by an extensive yoke of webbing and canvas which covers most of the back. The pouches are fastened across the waist with a clasp which secures and stabilizes the equipment. Weight would appear to be entirely supported by the shoulders and back, and adjustment of the harness is a fairly simple undertaking, being a question of lengthening or shortening the anchorage points of the ammunition pouches.

Whatever the configuration of the personal equipment accepted as a replacement for the 1958 pattern in British service, one fact is certain. Even though the design may be perfection itself it will at times be heartily loathed by the men who have to wear it! Only the infantryman who has experienced the sensation of floating or walking on air after removing his equipment at the end of a long and tiring march will be able to appreciate this. The command to 'Saddle up!' borrowed from our American cousins and meaning 'put your equipment on' is both apt and ironically humorous.

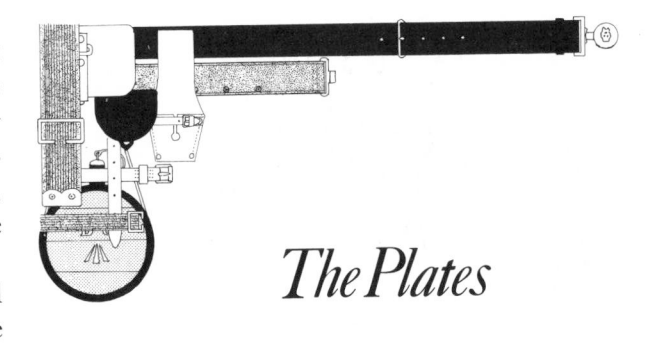

The Plates

A: The Pattern 1908 Web Infantry Equipment
(1) The rear view of the left-hand pouch or cartridge carrier showing the method of its attachment to the waistbelt, the method of attachment of the brace, and the bayonet-frog with the entrenching tool holder buckled in place.
(2) The head of the mattock-style entrenching tool with its web carrier.
(3) The kidney-section mess-tin issued with the

Respirators. At left is the current pattern. In the centre is the 'respirator, anti-gas, light', the first British Army mask to use an attached canister. Introduced in 1943, it served on until replaced by the current model in the late 1960s. On the right is the last pattern of box respirator to be used by the British Army. Still in use in the 1950s alongside the AG light model, it traced its history back to the light box respirator of the latter part of the Great War. The models of gas helmets and masks which preceded the light box respirator are too numerous and complex to mention here.

'08 pattern equipment in its canvas cover.

(4) The items of equipment special to troops armed with the .455in. Webley revolver. Shown here are the ammunition pouch, pistol case, pistol lanyard and the brace attachments.

(5) A lance-corporal of the 6th Bn., Gordon Highlanders in Full Marching Order, Western Front, 1918. This veteran soldier, 'out since Mons', wears insignia on his service dress tunic including the ribbons of the Military Medal and the 1914 Star, two good conduct badges, a wound stripe, overseas chevrons—one blue chevron for each year overseas with the red chevron indicating service overseas prior to December 1914— and a formation sign (three red bars) to indicate his battalion and company within the brigade.

(6) A private of the 8th Bn., Gloucestershire Regiment in Battle Order, Western Front, 1917. The device on the right forearm of his tunic is the 19th Division's 'Battle Badge'. A crimson silk butterfly, it was awarded to 'A' Company of the 8th Glosters by the divisional commander, General Tom Bridges, to reward gallant conduct during the heavy fighting of July 1917. Note regimental 'back badge' on steel helmet.

B: *The Pattern 1914 Leather Infantry Equipment*

(1) The waistbelt showing the snake-clasp buckle, the leather tongue of the buckle with the hole for rapid extension of the belt, the buckles at the rear of the belt for the attachment of the braces, the straps from the sides of the belt for the attachment of the base of the pack, and the bayonet, frog, entrenching tool helve and holder.

(2) One of the shoulder-braces with the buckle on the broad portion for the attachment of the upper edge of the pack.

(3) Enlarged detail of one of the ammunition pouches showing a bandolier of 50 rounds of small arms ammunition folded and inserted.

(4) A private soldier Lewis gunner of the 17th Bn., King's Royal Rifle Corps, Bapaume, Western Front, spring 1918. Our man is moving up to the line and is therefore in Marching Order. Of interest are the respirator carried on top of the pack in what was called the 'wading' position; the helmet secured to the pack by the valise straps; the 'kidney' mess-tin in its canvas cover; and the entrenching tool carrier fixed to the rear of the wearer instead of below the water-bottle.

eing in a rear area the magazine for the Lewis
un is off the gun and with its mates in the 'nose-
ag'-style carrier. Insignia visible include a Lewis
unner's proficiency badge on the left cuff, the
istinctive black shoulder title of the KRRC, the
lack cap badge on a red patch, and the red
iamond formation sign of 29th Division.

) A private of the 2nd/23rd Bn., The London
egiment, Macedonia, 1916. A member of a
erritorial Force battalion formed by the ex-
edient of raising two battalions on the cadre of
ie (1/23rd and 2/23rd), our subject shows the
ont view of the fighting order of the equipment.

: The Pattern 1937 Web Equipment

) Detail of the waistbelt buckle and the slides or
unners which kept it in position.

) Details of the brass press fastener and stud
ed to fasten pouches, etc. (this item was also
ed on the '08 pattern).

) A comparison of the basic and utility pouches.
 will be noted that the utility pouch was larger
an the basic pouch. Also seen is the attachment
r the yoke and the chest strap of the utility
ouch.

) A Bren light machine gun group of a 14th
rmy battalion in a defensive position, Burma
944/45. The Mark I Bren is mounted on its
ipod, which gave the gun a fixed-line capability
ost useful at night. Visible in the foreground are
e holdall with the second barrel and cleaning
quipment, a set of utility pouches, and the
ecial sling for the LMG. The 'No. 1', who is
cking the gun, has the spare parts wallet slung
om his right shoulder, and shows the front view
 the '37 pattern Battle Order without the
versack. The haversack is seen worn by the
o. 2'. He also has a set of utility pouches slung
ove his basic pouches, the second pattern
ater-bottle carrier, and an entrenching tool.

: The Pattern 1937 Web Equipment

) Detail of the brace attachment.
) Detail of the compass pocket.
) Pouch for the magazines of automatic pistols.
he pouch for Thompson SMG magazines was
milar to this item but of a size and shape to
commodate several Thompson box magazines.)
) Detail of cartridge carrier.

(5) Detail of the tongueless 'D' buckles and tags
used on the '37 pattern straps. (Identical items
were used on '08 pattern equipment also.)

(6) Lieutenant-Colonel, Hampshire Regiment,
North-West Frontier of India, 1938. This figure
is based on a picture of Lt.-Col. Ramsden, commanding the 1st Hampshires, who was photo-
graphed wearing the '37 pattern set shown.
Colonel Ramsden later became one of the desert
generals and commanded the 50th Division in
the North African campaign.

(7) The private of the King's Own Yorkshire
Light Infantry pictured here in 1940 shows in
detail the '37 pattern cartridge carriers in
'skeleton' order, and illustrates the carriage of the
final pattern of box respirator at the 'alert'. The
gas cape rolled on the shoulders afforded protection from blister gas when worn. Our soldier

Front left view, '58 pattern CEFO, showing carriage of respirator.

is typical of a sentry of the 'Phoney War' period. At this time hardly any insignia other than badges of rank were worn on battle-dress. Regimental identification was shown by means of a slip-on shoulder-strap patch with the title embroidered in black thread.

E: The 1942 Battle Jerkin
(1) Detail showing the machete in its sheath secured to the right side of the pack pocket by means of a strap and pocket. A 2in. mortar barrel could be secured in the same way.
(2) Detail of toggle and loop fastening used throughout the construction of the Jerkin. On the rear pockets the toggles were attached under the flaps to avoid snagging on barbed wire, etc.
(3) Detail of the pistol case which attached to the tab on the right hip of the jerkin.

Detail, '58 pattern pistol case.

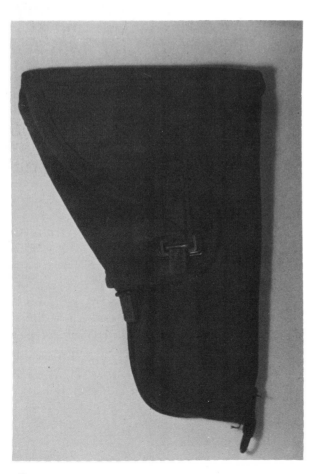

(4) A corporal of the Royal Berkshire Regiment attached to No. 6 Commando, 1st Special Service Brigade, 1944. No. 6 Commando were an Army commando and were part of the assault force of D-Day. Army commandos wore the badge of their 'parent' regiment in their green berets, and the NCO depicted wears the Commando title and the Combined Operations patch on the sleeve of his battledress. He is armed with a Mark III Sten 9mm machine carbine; note also the Fairbairn-Sykes fighting knife.
(5) A private of the 6th Bn., Green Howards, 69 Brigade, 50th (Northumbrian) Division, 1944. The 6th Green Howards were another unit ashore in the opening hours of D-Day. Note the whip-cord loops and the 'stops' on the shoulders; the ventilation panels at the waist; the 'respirator, anti-gas, light'; and the method of carriage of the bayonet and entrenching tool helve.

F: The 1944 Pattern Web Equipment
(1) Detail of the waistbelt.
(2) Detail of the machete.
(3) Detail of the pistol case.
(4) Detail of the bayonet-frog.
(5) Detail of the press fasteners used on the canteen cover and belt.
(6) A corporal of the Machine Gun Platoon, Support Company, 3rd Bn., Parachute Regiment, Suez, 1956. This NCO, a gun 'No. 1' wears '44 pattern Battle Order with the addition of a pistol carried on his right side. He carries a Vickers .303in. medium machine gun, with the dial sight in its leather case slung from his shoulder. In his left hand he carries his helmet and a 'liner' of belted ammunition. Note the green DZ patch of 3 Para on the shoulders of his Denison smock, and the green battalion lanyard round his left shoulder.
(7) A junior NCO patrol leader, 1st Royal Hampshires, Bentong, Malaya, 1954. Our subject shows the much-modified '44 pattern patrol equipment. Note the bulk of the pack with the spare clothing kept dry by being rolled in the poncho. Note also the extra canteen for rum; the US M2 .30 cal. carbine; the native *parang* knife; the operational identity band on the hat, and the shoulder patch of the 18th Independent Infantry Brigade.

: *The 1958 Pattern Web Equipment*

1) Compass and binocular cases.

2) Detail of the field pack, showing the hooks for attachment to the 'D' loops at the upper front of the yoke and the lower rear of the ammunition pouches.

3) A private of a Light Infantry battalion, Berlin Brigade, 1969. Our subject shows the rear of the Combat Equipment, Fighting Order. Note the carriage of the lightweight pick head and helve; the canteen in its pocket on the right hip; and the latest pattern respirator slung to hang on the left side. The helmet is not shown. Note the disruptive pattern material combat dress, the Berlin Brigade formation sign, and the 7.62mm general-purpose machine gun.

4) A warrant officer, Royal Irish Rangers, UK, 1974. Preparing for a session on the range, the warrant officer depicted shows the '58 pattern set with pistol case, binocular and compass case, belt and yoke only. Note the pocket for the second magazine and the stowage of the cleaning rod.

: *Future Developments*

2) and (3) Suggested design for a future infantry equipment based on the Finnish Army 'skeet jacket' style; the illustrations show the type of design described in the text. With equipment being manufactured from plastics an overprinted camouflage design should be possible. Note how the back is unencumbered so as to permit comfort within an APC, or to allow a rucksack or radio equipment to be worn with ease. A combination of pouches, canteen or pistol case can be attached to the hip 'pads'.

4) A sergeant, Parachute Regiment, 1980s. Our subject wears the recently adopted parachutists' smock, which has replaced the Denison. 'Subdued' insignia—an outcome of Vietnam and Northern Ireland—indicates rank, parachute brevet and a field force formation. His helmet is the pattern chosen to replace the Second World War parachutists' 'pot' and has a DPM cover. His equipment is the experimental vinyl-butyl

1958 pattern CEFO worn on active service; note that this soldier has fastened his cape carrier *above* the kidney pouches. *(Soldier Magazine)*

pattern described in the text, and he is armed with the latest generation of individual weapon and grenade. A folding shovel completes his battle-rig.

Notes sur les planches en couleur

A Equipements de l'an 1908: (1) Vue d'intérieur du côté gauche de la ceinture. (2) Pelle et son étui. (3) Gamelle dans sa housse. (4) Equipement du pistolet. (5) Lance-Corporal, 6th Bn. Gordon Highlanders, France, 1918. Insignes de la manche gauche: titre du régiment en cuivre; barres rouges indiquant qu'il s'agit d'un bataillon au sein d'une brigade; chevron de rang; chevrons de bonne conduite; barre de blessure. Sur la manchette droite, des chevrons rouges et bleus indiquent la durée du service. (6) Private, 8th Bn. Gloucestershire Regiment, France, 1917, les équipements vus de derrière. Notez l'insigne porté sur l'arrière du casque, particularité du régiment des Gloucesters; et le papillon rouge sur la manche, rappelant un combat difficile en juillet 1917 dans lequel s'est battue la Compagnie 'A' de ce bataillon.

B Equipements de l'an 1914: (1 à 3) Ceinture, attache d'épaule et un détail agrandi de la cartouchière (4) Private, 17th Bn., King's Royal Rifle Corps, France, 1918; il porte l'équipement complet de marche, est armé d'une mitrailleuse Lewis et porte une cartouchière sous forme de 'seau' en toile, il porte également le carreau rouge de la 29ème division. (5) Private, 2nd/23rd Bn. The London Regiment, 1916, l'équipement étant vu de devant.

C Equipement de l'an 1937 porté par les équipiers d'une mitrailleuse Bren, en Birmanie, 1944 à 45: (1 et 2) Détail de la boucle de la ceinture et des agrafes utilisées sur les sangles. (3) Types de sacoches; à gauche la 'basic' et à droite la 'utility'. Au gros plan, le 'hold-all' contenant des outils, du matériel de nettoyage, un canon de rechange pour la Bren est par terre à côté d'un jeu de sacoches 'utility' remplies de munitions. L'homme à gauche en porte un autre jeu par dessus ses sacoches 'basic'; l'homme à droite porte suspendue à son épaule la trousse de pièces détachées.

D Equipement de l'an 1937: (1) sangle pour relier la ceinture à l'attache de l'épaule. (2) étui de compas. (3) cartouchière pour pistolet automatique. (4) 'Cartridge-carrier' qui a remplacé la 'basic pouch' pour le personnel autre que l'infanterie de combat. (5) détail des boucles et agrafes de sangles. (6) Lieutenant-Colonel, Hampshire Regiment sur la frontière nord-ouest de l'Inde en 1938, portant le type d'équipement distribué aux officiers en 1937. (7) Private, King's Own Yorkshire Light Infantry, Royaume-Uni, 1940, équipé de cartouchières, trousse pour masque à gaz et cape anti-gaz enroulée.

E 1942 Battle Jerkin: (1) Machette sur le côté droit du compartiment supérieur arrière. (2) Détail du bouton en forme de cabillot. (3) Etui à pistolet attaché à une patte sur la hanche droite. (4) Corporal, Royal Berkshire Regiment, servant avec le Commando No 6 en Normandie, le Jour-J. (5) Private, 6th Bn. Green Howards, 50ème division; Normandie, le Jour-J. Ces deux tableaux montrent le devant et le derrière du 'justaucorps de bataille' à amples poches; cet excellent article vestimentaire était rarement vu au combat après avoir été utilisé par les troupes d'assaut le Jour-J—triomphe du conservatisme militaire sur le bon sens.

F Equipement de l'an 1944: (1 à 5) Détail de la ceinture, la machette, l'étui à pistolet, le porte-baionnette et les agrafes. (6) Caporal, 3ème Bataillon du Régiment de Parachutistes à Suez en 1956. Ce sous-officier du peloton mitrailleur porte la mitrailleuse Vickers et en porte les objectifs dans un étui en cuir suspendu à son épaule. Le cordon vert et la plaque appliquée sur la manche identifient le bataillon. (7) Chef de patrouille, 1st Bn. Royal Hampshires, Malaisie, 1954. Il a ajouté à son équipement un couteau malais et une carabine américaine.

G Equipement de l'an 1958: (1 et 2) Etuis à compas et à jumelles et sacoche de campagne. (3) Soldat de la 'Light Infantry' à Berlin en 1969, montrant le 'combat equipment, fighting order' vu de dos. (4) Warrant Officer, Royal Irish Rangers, en 1974, montrant un étui à pistolet.

H L'équipement des années 80, tel que pourrait le porter un sergent du Parachute Regiment. (1 et 3) sont des dessins proposés par l'auteur pour un équipement amélioré basé sur des modèles finlandais.

Farbtafeln

A 1908er Ausrüstung: (1) Blick in die innere linke Seite der Koppel. (2) Spaten und seine Hülle. (3) Kochgeschirr in der Hülle. (4) Pistolenausrüstung. (5) Lance-corporal, 6th Bn., Gordon Highlanders, Frankreich 19.. Abzeichen am linken Arm: Name des Regiments in Messing, rote Streif.. das Bataillon innerhalb der Brigade anzeigend; Rangarmwinkel; Armwink.. für gutes Verhalten; Verwundungsstreifen. Am rechten Armaufschlag ro.. und blaue Winkel, die die Dienstlänge kennzeichnen. (6) Private, 8th B.. Gloucestershire Regiment, Frankreich 1917, die Rückseite der Ausrüstu.. zeigend. Bemerke das Abzeichen auf der Helmrückseite, eine regimenta.. Eigenart der Gloucesters; und ein rotes Schmetterling-Armabzeichen, d.. an einen harten Kampf im Juli 1917 der 'A' Kompanie dieses Batailla.. erinnert.

B 1914er Ausrüstung: (1–3) Koppel, Schulterriemen und vergrösserte Ansic.. der Gürteltasche. (4) Private, 17th Bn., King's Royal Rifle Corps, Frankrei.. 1918; er trägt volle Marschausrüstung, er trägt ein Lewis Maschinengewe.. und einen Segeltuch 'Eimer' mit dessen Magazinen und trägt das ro.. Rautenabzeichen der 29. Division. (5) Private, 2nd/23rd Bn., The Lond.. Regiment, Macedonien 1916, die Vorderansicht der Ausrüstung zeigend.

C Die 1937er Ausrüstung von einer Bren-Maschinengewehrmannsch.. getragen, 1944–45 in Burma: (1, 2) Einzelausschnitt einer Koppelschlie.. und Druckknöpfe, benutzt an Schulterriemen. (3) Koppeltaschentype.. links, 'basic' und rechts, 'utility'. (4) Im Vordergrund, die 'hold-all' m.. Werkzeugen, Reinigungsgegenständen und Reservekolben für das Bren lie.. in der Nähe eines Satzes der 'utility' Taschen gefüllt mit Magazinen. D.. Mann auf der linken Seits trägt einen weiteren Satz über seine 'basic' Tasc.. geschlungen; der Mann rechts hat die Tasche mit den Bren–Ersatzteil.. über seine Schulter geschlungen.

D 1937er Ausrüstung: (1) Befestigung der Koppel zum Schulterriemen. (.. Kompasstasche. (3) Magazinbeutel für die Automatische Pistole. (.. 'Cartridge carrier' der die 'basic pouch' für das Personal ausser der Kampf.. fanterie ersetzt hat. (5) Genaue Ansicht des Schliessen und Riemende.. (6) Lieutenant-colonel, Hampshire Regiment, Nordwest-Grenze von Indi.. 1938, einen 1937er Offiziers-Ausrüstungssatz tragend. (7) Private, Kin.. Own Yorkshire Light Infantry, UK 1940, mit 'Patronenträger', G.. maskenbeutel und gerolltem Gasumhang.

E 1942 Battle Jerkin: (1) Machete an der rechten Seite im hinteren Fa.. oben. (2) Genaue Ansicht eines Knebelknopfs. (3) Pistolenhalfter an e.. Schlaufe an der rechten Hüfte befestigt. (4) Corporal, Royal Berksh.. Regiment, dienend mit Nr. 6 Kommando; Normandie, Tag der Landun.. (5) Private, 6th Bn. Green Howards, 50. Division; Normandie, Tag d.. Landung. Diese zwei Gemälde zeigen die Vorder- und Rückenansicht e.. geräumigen 'Kampfwames', diese ausgezeichnete Ausrüstung wurde selt.. im Einsatz gesehen, nachdem die Angriffstruppen es am Tag der Landu.. benutzten, ein Sieg des militärischen Konservatismus über den gesund.. Menschenverstand.

F 1944er Ausrüstung: (1–5) Genaue Ansicht der Koppel, der Machete, .. Pistolenhalfters, der Bajonetthalterung und der Druckknöpfe. (6) Corpor.. 3rd Bn., Parachute Regiment, Suez 1956. Dieser Unteroffizier des Masch.. gewehrzuges trägt das Vickers Maschinengewehr und hat dessen Visier .. einem Lederhalter über seine Schulter geschlungen. Grüne Schulterkord.. und Armflecken identifizieren das Bataillon. (7) Patrouillenführer, 1st B.. Royal Hampshires, Malaya 1954. Er hat seiner Ausrüstung einen e.. heinischen *parang* und einen US-Karabiner hinzugefügt.

G 1958er Ausrüstung: (1–2) Kompass- und Feldstechertaschen und Fe.. tasche. (3) Light Infantry Soldat, Berlin 1969, die Rückenansicht der 'comb.. equipment, fighting order' zeigend. (4) Warrant Officer, Royal Irish Range.. 1974, den Pistolenhalfter zeigend.

H Die Ausrüstung der 1980er, wie sie von einem Feldwebel des Parach.. Regiment getragen werden könnte. (1 und 3) sind die vom Author v.. geschlagenen Entwürfe für eine verbesserte Ausrüstung basiert auf finnisch.. Mustern.